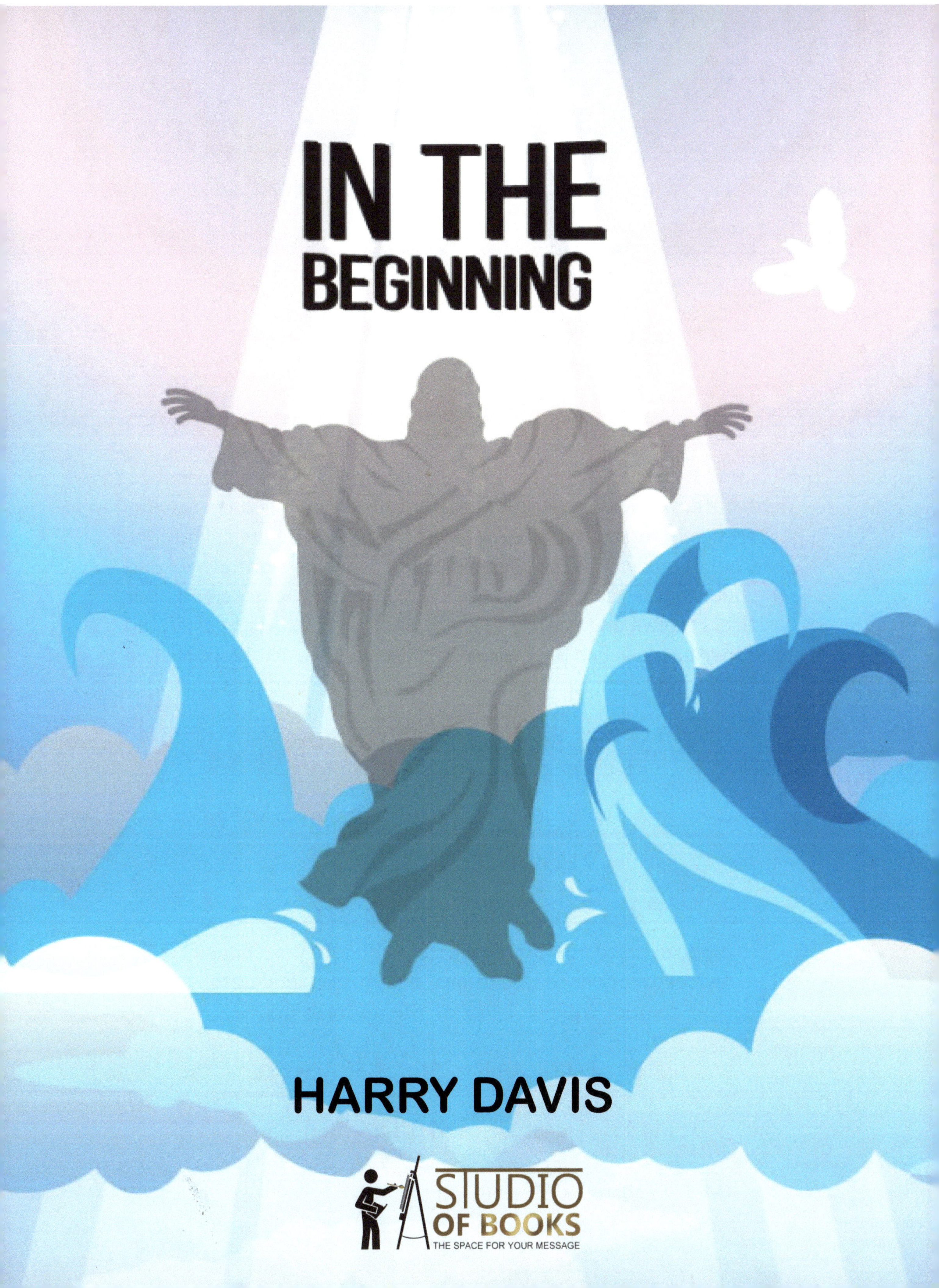

IN THE BEGINNING

HARRY DAVIS

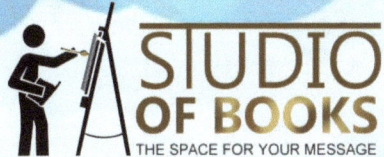

Copyright © 2024 by Harry Davis

All rights reserved. No part of this publication may be reproduced, distributed, or transmitted in any form or by any means, including photocopying, recording, or other electronic or mechanical methods, without the prior written permission of the copyright owner and the publisher, except in the case of brief quotations embodied in critical reviews and certain other noncommercial uses permitted by copyright law. For permission requests, write to the publisher, "Attention: Permissions Coordinator," to the address below.

Studio of Books LLC
5900 Balcones Drive Suite 100
Austin, Texas 78731
www.studioofbooks.org
Hotline: (254) 800-1183

Ordering Information:
Special discounts are available on quantity purchases by corporations, associations, and others. For details, contact the publisher at the address above.

Printed in the United States of America.

ISBN-13: Hardcover   978-1-964864-28-0

Library of Congress Control Number: 2024915525

A long, long time ago, almighty God created the heaven and earth. Then, God looked down upon the earth and saw that the earth was without shape, it was very dark, and there was nothing on the earth to behold. It was empty.

Then God began to speak to the earth, and He said let there be light on the earth, and there was light. And He divided the light from the darkness. He called the light day, and the darkness He called night.

Then God said let there be signs for seasons and days and years such as winter, spring, summer, and fall. Then God began to speak forth other things into existence.

God saith let there be areas of dry land and let there be areas of water called seas to separate the land. Then God said, let there be grass upon the earth and plants and herb and trees yielding fruit after its own kind, let there be cattle, and beast and creeping things upon the earth and fowls of the air and let them reproduce after their own kind and replenish the earth.

God then said let there be stars in the sky and let there be a sun in the sky to give heat to the earth and a moon in the sky to give light at night.

Then God said now that I have created the heaven and earth and all the imaginable cattle of the field, the plants and herbs of the ground, the beasts of the land, the creeping things upon the earth, and the fowls of the air. Then God said, I am going to make one final creation.

God said I will make man in my image and likeness, giving him dominion over everything I have made. Over the fish of the sea, and over the fowl of the air and the cattle of the field, and over the creeping thing that creeps over the earth.

So, God created man in his image.
He formed man from the dust of the earth.
He then breathed into man's nostrils the breath of life,
and man became a living soul. God called the man
"Adam."

Then God saw everything that
he created was not only good but very good.

After God gave Adam his name, He brought all the beasts of the field and the fowls of the air and the cattle of the field to Adam, and He said to Adam, whatever you name them, this is what they will be called, so Adam gave them all names and God was pleased.

God made a mate for every beast of the field, creeping thing, cattle of the ground, and fowls of the air and everything that lives in the water.
He creates a male and female.
He saw how happy they were together.

But when God looked at Adam, He saw man was all alone. He said it is not good for man to be alone. Since I had created a mate for all the beast, cattle, the fowls of the air, and everything that swims in the water, I will make a mate for Adam.

Then God caused a deep sleep to come upon Adam, and Adam slept. While Adam slept, God operated on Adam and took out one of his ribs. God then closed Adam's body back up. God performed the first operation known in the bible when He operated on Adam. Adam felt no pain while being operated on by God.

God woke up Adam from his deep sleep. When he arose, he saw one of God's most beautiful creation standing beside him.

Then God said, therefore shall a man
leave his father and mother
and join himself unto his wife,
and the two shall become one flesh.

Then Adam said to his soulmate and helper,
since you were taken out of my rib,
you are bones of my bones and flesh of my flesh,
you shall be called woman.

God said to Adam; this is your soulmate and helper. I have made her from your rib; not from your head for her to be over you, not from your feet for you to step on her, but from near your side to be equal to you, and from under your arm to be protected by you, and from near your heart to be loved by you. God went on to say, "Adam, cherish her, respect her, and care for her just like you would care for yourself."

Then God said to the man and woman, have children,
be fruitful and multiply and fill the earth,
just like I have blessed the cattle of the field,
the beast of the field, the creeping things,
the fowls of the air and all that swim in
the waters to be fruitful and multiply.

Then Adam called his wife Eve because she was the mother of all living.

www.ingramcontent.com/pod-product-compliance
Lightning Source LLC
Chambersburg PA
CBHW041411010526
44107CB00015B/1136